PMP® Pocket Guide

The Ultimate PMP Exam Cheat Sheets

For the *PMBOK® Guide* - Fifth Edition

Belinda Fremouw
PMP, PMI-RMP, PMI-SP, PgMP, PMI-ACP, CAPM

PassionatePM.com
BelindaFremouw.com

TABLE OF CONTENTS

To my students…
Thank you for always teaching me so much more than I could ever teach you

Introduction

This PMP Pocket Guide is designed to give you a quick summary of all of the key concepts that you will need to know to feel confident going into the PMP (Project Management Professional) exam. **It is intended to be a supplement to your PMP exam prep course or self-study program and not a stand-alone preparation tool.**

The PMP exam is administered by the Project Management Institute (PMI). Qualified, experienced project managers (PMs) can apply to PMI to take the exam. The exam is administered at Prometric locations globally. To find a location near you visit Prometric.com/PMI.

The PMP exam is based on PMI's *PMBOK® Guide* and "other relevant sources". While the *PMBOK® Guide* is a great cure for insomnia, it is not the most interesting or comprehensive method to prepare for the exam.

Within the *PMBOK® Guide*, PMI presents the Project Management Framework, which you will find on the following two pages. Please note that there are:

- Ten **Knowledge Areas**
- Five **Process Groups** (groups of related processes, not phases)
- Forty-seven **Processes**, each associated with a knowledge area and a process group

For each of the 47 processes, there are:

- **Inputs** to that process
- **Tools and Techniques** that may be used during that process
- **Outputs** from that process, many of which become inputs to other processes

These are called "ITTOs". On pages 4, 5, 6 and 7, you will see all of the ITTOs for all 47 processes. They are organized by knowledge area. I do not recommend memorizing all of the ITTOs; by understanding each of the 47 processes, however, the ITTOs for that process will be more intuitive. On page 8, I provide you with a list of the common ITTOs: those that you have to understand although it is not critical to memorize which processes have them and which do not.

All of the processes are described in detail starting on page 38.

As you are preparing for your exam, if you get to a page in this book that appears to be new information, cross-reference the topic with your courseware, self-study materials, or the *PMBOK® Guide* for more information.

For additional study materials, free resources, or to enroll in a convenient class, visit us at PassionatePM.com.

| KNOWLEDGE AREAS | PROCESS GROUPS | |
	Initiating 2 processes 13% of exam	Planning 24 processes 24% of exam
Integration	• Develop Project Charter	• Develop Project Management Plan
Scope		• Plan Scope Management • Collect Requirements • Define Scope • Create WBS
Time		• Plan Schedule Management • Define Activities • Sequence Activities • Estimate Activity Resources • Estimate Activity Durations • Develop Schedule
Cost		• Plan Cost Management • Estimate Costs • Determine Budget
Quality		• Plan Quality Management
Human Resource		• Plan Human Resource Management
Communications		• Plan Communications Management
Risk		• Plan Risk Management • Identify Risks • Perform Qualitative Risk Analysis • Perform Quantitative Risk Analysis • Plan Risk Responses
Procurement		• Plan Procurement Management
Stakeholder	• Identify Stakeholders	• Plan Stakeholder Management

Project Management Institute, *A Guide to the Project Management Body of Knowledge, (PMBOK® Guide)* – Fifth Edition, Project Management Institute Inc., 2013, Table 3–1, pg 61.

PROCESS GROUPS		
Executing 8 processes 31% of exam	**Monitoring and Controlling** 11 processes 25% of exam	**Closing** 2 processes 7% of exam
• Direct and Manage Project Work	• Monitor and Control Project Work • Perform Integrated Change Control	• Close Project or Phase
	• Validate Scope • Control Scope	
	• Control Schedule	
	• Control Costs	
• Perform Quality Assurance	• Control Quality	
• Acquire Project Team • Develop Project Team • Manage Project Team		
• Manage Communications	• Control Communications	
	• Control Risks	
• Conduct Procurements	• Control Procurements	• Close Procurements
• Manage Stakeholder Engagement	• Control Stakeholder Engagement	

PROCESSES are named in a verb-noun format (ex: Develop Schedule)

PROCESS GROUPS are groups of related processes, <u>not</u> phases, and can occur concurrently and iteratively

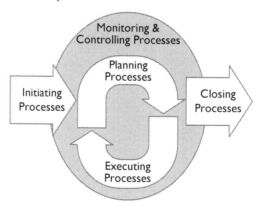

3

	Process	Inputs	Tools & Techniques	Outputs
INTEGRATION	**Develop Project Charter**	1. Project statement of work 2. Business case 3. Agreements 4. EEF 5. OPA	1. Expert judgment 2. Facilitation techniques	1. Project charter
	Develop Project Management Plan	1. Project charter 2. Outputs from other processes 3. EEF 4. OPA	1. Expert judgment 2. Facilitation techniques	1. Project management plan
	Direct and Manage Project Work	1. Project management plan 2. Approved change requests 3. EEF 4. OPA	1. Expert judgment 2. Project management information system 3. Meetings	1. Deliverables 2. Work performance data 3. Change requests 4. Project management plan updates 5. Project documents updates
	Monitor and Control Project Work	1. Project management plan 2. Schedule forecasts 3. Cost forecasts 4. Validated changes 5. Work performance information 6. EEF 7. OPA	1. Expert judgment 2. Analytical techniques 3. Project management information system 4. Meetings	1. Change requests 2. Work performance reports 3. Project management plan updates 4. Project documents updates
	Perform Integrated Change Control	1. Project management plan 2. Work performance reports 3. Change requests 4. EEF 5. OPA	1. Expert judgment 2. Meetings 3. Change control tools	1. Approved change requests 2. Change log 3. Project management plan updates 4. Project documents updates
	Close Project or Phase	1. Project management plan 2. Accepted deliverables 3. OPA	1. Expert judgment 2. Analytical techniques 3. Meetings	1. Final product, service, or result transition 2. OPA updates
SCOPE	**Plan Scope Management**	1. Project management plan 2. Project charter 3. EEF 4. OPA	1. Expert judgment 2. Meetings	1. Scope management plan 2. Requirements management plan
	Collect Requirements	1. Scope management plan 2. Requirements management plan 3. Stakeholder management plan 4. Project charter 5. Stakeholder register	1. Interviews 2. Focus groups 3. Facilitated workshops 4. Group creativity techniques 5. Group decision-making techniques 6. Questionnaires and surveys 7. Observations 8. Prototypes 9. Benchmarking 10. Context diagram 11. Document analysis	1. Requirements documentation 2. Requirements traceability matrix
	Define Scope	1. Scope management plan 2. Project charter 3. Requirements documentation 4. OPA	1. Expert judgment 2. Product analysis 3. Alternatives analysis 4. Facilitated workshops	1. Project scope statement 2. Project documents updates
	Create WBS	1. Scope management plan 2. Project scope statement 3. Requirements documentation 4. EEF 5. OPA	1. Decomposition 2. Expert judgment	1. Scope baseline 2. Project documents updates
	Validate Scope	1. Project management plan 2. Requirements documentation 3. Requirements traceability matrix 4. Verified deliverables 5. Work performance data	1. Inspection 2. Group decision-making techniques	1. Accepted deliverables 2. Change requests 3. Work performance information 4. Project documents updates
	Control Scope	1. Project management plan 2. Requirements documentation 3. Requirements traceability matrix 4. Work performance data 5. OPA	1. Variance analysis	1. Work performance information 2. Change requests 3. Project management plan updates 4. Project documents updates 5. OPA updates

	Process	Inputs	Tools & Techniques	Outputs
TIME	**Plan Schedule Management**	1. Project management plan 2. Project charter 3. EEF 4. OPA	1. Expert judgment 2. Analytical techniques 3. Meetings	1. Schedule management plan
	Define Activities	1. Schedule management plan 2. Scope baseline 3. EEF 4. OPA	1. Decomposition 2. Rolling wave planning 3. Expert judgment	1. Activity list 2. Activity attributes 3. Milestone list
	Sequence Activities	1. Schedule management plan 2. Activity list 3. Activity attributes 4. Milestone list 5. Project scope statement 6. EEF 7. OPA	1. Precedence diagramming method (PDM) 2. Dependency determination 3. Leads and lags	1. Project schedule network diagrams 2. Project documents updates
	Estimate Activity Resources	1. Schedule management plan 2. Activity list 3. Activity attributes 4. Resource calendars 5. Risk register 6. Activity cost estimates 7. EEF 10. OPA	1. Expert judgment 2. Alternative analysis 3. Published estimating data 4. Bottom–up estimating 5. Project management software	1. Activity resource requirements 2. Resource breakdown structure 3. Project documents updates
	Estimate Activity Durations	1. Schedule management plan 2. Activity list 3. Activity attributes 4. Activity resource requirements 5. Resource calendars 6. Project scope statement 7. Risk register 8. Resource breakdown structure 9. EEF 10. OPA	1. Expert judgment 2. Analogous estimating 3. Parametric estimating 4. Three–point estimating 5. Group decision–making techniques 4. Reserve analysis	1. Activity duration estimates 2. Project documents updates
	Develop Schedule	1. Schedule management plan 2. Activity list 3. Activity attributes 4. Project schedule network diagrams 5. Activity resource requirements 6. Resource calendars 7. Activity duration estimates 8. Project scope statement 9. Risk register 10.Project staff assignments 11.Resource breakdown structure 12.EEF 13. OPA	1. Schedule network analysis 2. Critical path method 3. Critical chain method 4. Resource optimization techniques 5. Modeling techniques 6. Leads and lags 7. Schedule compression 8. Scheduling tool	1. Schedule baseline 2. Project schedule 3. Schedule data 4. Project calendars 5. Project management plan updates 6. Project documents updates
	Control Schedule	1. Project management plan 2. Project schedule 3. Work performance data 4. Project calendars 5. Schedule data 6. OPA	1. Performance reviews 2. Project management software 3. Resource optimization techniques 4. Modeling techniques 5. Leads and lags 6. Schedule compression 7. Scheduling tool	1. Work performance information 2. Schedule forecasts 3. Change requests 4. Project management plan updates 5. Project documents updates 6. OPA updates
COST	**Plan Cost Management**	1. Project management plan 2. Project charter 3. EEF 4. OPA	1. Expert judgment 2. Analytical techniques 3. Meetings	1. Cost management plan
	Estimate Costs	1. Cost management plan 2. Human resource management plan 3. Scope baseline 4. Project schedule 5. Risk register 6. EEF 7. OPA	1. Expert judgment 2. Analogous estimating 3. Parametric estimating 4. Bottom–up estimating 5. Three–point estimating 6. Reserve analysis 7. Cost of quality 8. Project management software 9. Vendor bid analysis 10.Group decision–making techniques	1. Activity cost estimates 2. Basis of estimates 3. Project documents updates
	Determine Budget	1. Cost management plan 2. Scope baseline 3. Activity cost estimates 4. Basis of estimates 5. Project schedule 6. Resource calendars 7. Risk register 8. Agreements 9. OPA	1. Cost aggregation 2. Reserve analysis 3. Expert judgment 4. Historical relationships 5. Funding limit reconciliation	1. Cost baseline 2. Project funding requirements 3. Project documents updates
	Control Costs	1. Project management plan 2. Project funding requirements 3. Work performance data 4. OPA	1. Earned value management 2. Forecasting 3. To-complete performance index (TCPI) 4. Performance reviews 5. Project management software 6. Reserve analysis	1. Work performance information 2. Cost forecasts 3. Change requests 4. Project management plan updates 5. Project documents updates 6. OPA updates

	Process	Inputs	Tools & Techniques	Outputs
QUALITY	Plan Quality Management	1. Project management plan 2. Stakeholder register 3. Risk register 4. Requirements documentation 5. EEF 6. OPA	1. Cost-benefit analysis 2. Cost of quality 3. Seven basic quality tools 4. Benchmarking 5. Design of experiments 6. Statistical sampling 7. Additional quality planning tools 8. Meetings	1. Quality management plan 2. Process improvement plan 3. Quality metrics 4. Quality checklists 5. Project documents updates
	Perform Quality Assurance	1. Quality management plan 2. Process improvement plan 3. Quality metrics 4. Quality control measurements 5. Project documents	1. Quality management and control tools 2. Quality audits 3. Process analysis	1. Change requests 2. Project management plan updates 3. Project documents updates 4. OPA updates
	Control Quality	1. Project management plan 2. Quality metrics 3. Quality checklists 4. Work performance data 5. Approved change requests 6. Deliverables 7. Project documents 8. OPA	1. Seven basic quality tools 2. Statistical sampling 3. Inspection 4. Approved change requests review	1. Quality control measurements 2. Validated changes 3. Verified deliverables 4. Work performance information 5. Change requests 6. Project management plan updates 7. Project documents updates 8. OPA updates
HUMAN RESOURCE	Plan Human Resource Management	1. Project management plan 2. Activity resource requirements 3. EEF 4. OPA	1. Organization charts and position descriptions 2. Networking 3. Organizational theory 4. Expert judgment 5. Meetings	1. Human resource management plan
	Acquire Project Team	1. Human resource management plan 2. EEF 3. OPA	1. Pre-assignment 2. Negotiation 3. Acquisition 4. Virtual teams 5. Multi-criteria decision analysis	1. Project staff assignments 2. Resource calendars 3. Project management plan updates
	Develop Project Team	1. Human resource management plan 2. Project staff assignments 3. Resource calendars	1. Interpersonal skills 2. Training 3. Team-building activities 4. Ground rules 5. Colocation 6. Recognition and rewards 7. Personnel assessment tools	1. Team performance assessments 2. EEF updates
	Manage Project Team	1. Human resource management plan 2. Project staff assignments 3. Team performance assessments 4. Issue log 5. Work performance reports 6. OPA	1. Observation and conversation 2. Project performance appraisals 3. Conflict management 4. Interpersonal skills	1. Change requests 2. Project management plan updates 3. Project documents updates 4. EEF updates 5. OPA updates
COMMUNICATION	Plan Communications Management	1. Project management plan 2. Stakeholder register 3. EEF 4. OPA	1. Communication requirements analysis 2. Communication technology 3. Communication models 4. Communication methods 5. Meetings	1. Communications management plan 2. Project documents updates
	Manage Communications	1. Communications management plan 2. Work performance reports 3. EEF 4. OPA	1. Communication technology 2. Communication models 3. Communication methods 4. Information management systems 5. Performance reporting	1. Project communications 2. Project management plan updates 3. Project documents updates 4. OPA updates
	Control Communications	1. Project management plan 2. Project communications 3. Issue log 4. Work performance data 5. OPA	1. Information management systems 2. Expert judgment 3. Meetings	1. Work performance information 2. Change requests 3. Project management plan updates 4. Project documents updates 5. OPA updates

	Process	Inputs	Tools & Techniques	Outputs
RISK	**Plan Risk Management**	1. Project management plan 2. Project charter 3. Stakeholder register 4. EEF 5. OPA	1. Analytical techniques 2. Expert judgment 3. Meetings	1. Risk management plan
	Identify Risks	1. Risk management plan 2. Cost management plan 3. Schedule management plan 4. Quality management plan 5. HR management plan 6. Scope baseline 7. Activity cost estimates 8. Activity duration estimates 9. Stakeholder register 10. Project documents 11. Procurement documents 12. EEF 13. OPA	1. Documentation reviews 2. Information gathering techniques 3. Checklist analysis 4. Assumptions analysis 5. Diagramming techniques 6. SWOT analysis 7. Expert judgment	1. Risk register
	Perform Qualitative Risk Analysis	1. Risk management plan 2. Scope baseline 3. Risk register 4. EEF 5. OPA	1. Risk probability and impact assessment 2. Probability and impact matrix 3. Risk data quality assessment 4. Risk categorization 5. Risk urgency assessment 6. Expert judgment	1. Project documents updates
	Perform Quantitative Risk Analysis	1. Risk management plan 2. Cost management plan 3. Schedule management plan 4. Risk register 5. EEF 6. OPA	1. Data gathering and representation techniques 2. Quantitative risk analysis and modeling techniques 3. Expert judgment	1. Project documents updates
	Plan Risk Responses	1. Risk management plan 2. Risk register	1. Strategies for negative risks (threats) 2. Strategies for positive risks (opportunities) 3. Contingent response strategies 4. Expert judgment	1. Project management plan updates 2. Project documents updates
	Control Risks	1. Project management plan 2. Risk register 3. Work performance data 4. Work performance reports	1. Risk reassessment 2. Risk audits 3. Variance and trend analysis 4. Technical performance measurement 5. Reserve analysis 6. Meetings	1. Work performance information 2. Change requests 3. Project management plan updates 4. Project documents updates 5. OPA updates
PROCUREMENT	**Plan Procurement Management**	1. Project management plan 2. Requirements documentation 3. Risk register 4. Activity resource requirements 5. Project schedule 6. Activity cost estimates 7. Stakeholder register 8. EEF 9. OPA	1. Make-or-buy analysis 2. Expert judgment 3. Market research 4. Meetings	1. Project management plan 2. Procurement statement of work 3. Procurement documents 4. Source selection criteria 5. Make-or-buy decisions 6. Change requests 7. Project documents updates
	Conduct Procurements	1. Procurement management plan 2. Procurement documents 3. Source selection criteria 4. Seller proposals 5. Project documents 6. Make-or-buy decisions 7. Procurement statement of work 8. OPA	1. Bidder conference 2. Proposal evaluation techniques 3. Independent estimates 4. Expert judgment 5. Advertising 6. Analytical techniques 7. Procurement negotiations	1. Selected sellers 2. Agreements 3. Resource calendars 4. Change requests 5. Project management plan updates 6. Project documents updates
	Control Procurements	1. Project management plan 2. Procurement documents 3. Agreements 4. Approved change requests 5. Work performance reports 6. Work performance data	1. Contract change control system 2. Procurement performance reviews 3. Inspections and audits 4. Performance reporting 5. Payment systems 6. Claims administration 7. Records management system	1. Work performance information 2. Change requests 3. Project management plan updates 4. Project documents updates 5. OPA updates
	Close Procurements	1. Project management plan 2. Procurement documents	1. Procurement audits 2. Procurement negotiations 3. Records management system	1. Closed procurements 2. OPA updates
STAKEHOLDER	**Identify Stakeholders**	1. Project charter 2. Procurement documents 3. EEF 4. OPA	1. Stakeholder analysis 2. Expert judgment 3. Meetings	1. Stakeholder register
	Plan Stakeholder Management	1. Project management plan 2. Stakeholder register 3. EEF 4. OPA	1. Expert judgment 2. Meetings 3. Analytical techniques	1. Stakeholder management plan 2. Project documents updates
	Manage Stakeholder Engagement	1. Stakeholder management plan 2. Communications management plan 3. Change log 4. OPA	1. Communication methods 2. Interpersonal skills 3. Management skills	1. Issue log 2. Change requests 3. Project management plan updates 4. Project documents updates 5. OPA updates
	Control Stakeholder Engagement	1. Project management plan 2. Issue log 3. Work performance data 4. Project documents	1. Information management systems 2. Expert judgment 3. Meetings	1. Work performance information 2. Change requests 3. Project management plan updates 4. Project documents updates 5. OPA updates

PM Foundation

Definitions

Project – A temporary endeavor undertaken to create a unique product, service, or result.

Program – A collection of related projects managed in a cohesive and consistent manner.

Portfolio – A collection of projects and programs that may or may not be related.

Progressive Elaboration – An iterative approach to project management, where the work is elaborated one phase at a time, adding information as more details are understood.

Triple Constraint – Traditional project constraints of scope, time, and cost are related in that if one changes, more than likely (but not always), the others will be effected.

Project Life Cycle – The phases of the project work, allowing for increased control and management.

Project Management Office – A centralized coordinator of projects or programs that may have roles and responsibilities that vary by organization.

Project Life Cycle Types

Predictive – Scope, time, and cost are determined as early in the life cycle as possible -- known as fully plan-driven life cycles.

Iterative / Incremental – Project phases or iterations that intentionally repeat as the team's understanding increases.

Adaptive – Utilized to respond to high levels of change and increased stakeholder involvement -- known as agile or change-drive approaches, such as Scrum, XP, or Lean.

Project Management Office (PMO) Types

Supportive PMO – Low control -- provides templates, lessons learned, and training to the project team -- serves as a project repository.

Controlling PMO – Moderate control -- provides support, implements controls and procedures, and monitors the projects' compliance with the defined framework.

Directive PMO – High control -- directly manages the projects.

PM Foundation

Organizational Types

Functional – Classical hierarchical structure where each employee has one clear manager or supervisor and employees are grouped by the function they perform. No recognized project management.

Weak Matrix – Matrix that more closely resembles a functional organization. Use of coordinators or expeditors versus project managers.

Matrix / Balanced Matrix – Project staff report administratively to a functional manager and dotted-line to a project manager. Communication is more complex and must travel both horizontally and vertically.

Strong Matrix – Matrix that more closely resembles a projectized organization.

Projectized – Majority of the organization's resources are involved in project work generally for the benefit of an external customer. PM has increased authority and control.

Composite – May involve components of other structures at various levels and may have full-time staff from different functional departments.

Project-Based Organization (PBO) – Creates temporary systems for carrying out their project work, with an objective to minimize bureaucracy.

Project Roles

Project Manager – Individual assigned by the performing organization to achieve the project objectives.

Project Sponsor – Individual who authorizes the project and the project funding.

Stakeholders – Individuals or organizations that are either involved in the project or are affected by a decision, activity or outcome of the project.

Sellers – Vendors, suppliers, contractors, and/or sub-contractors external to the organization that provide products or services.

Project Management Staff – Members who perform project management activities, such as scheduling, budgeting, reporting and control, risk management, etc.

Project Staff – Members who carry out the work of completing the project deliverables.

Common ITTOs

Common Inputs

Project Management Plan – Mandatory "how–to" guide for the project, encompassing the project performance baselines (scope, schedule, and cost) and any subsidiary plans.

Project Documents – Project documentation such as the risk register, issue log, change log, project correspondence.

Work Performance Data – Raw information resulting from the project activities (see page 11).

Enterprise Environmental Factors – Internal and external factors that can influence a project's success.

Organizational Process Assets – Procedures, guidelines, templates, lessons learned, historical information, past project files.

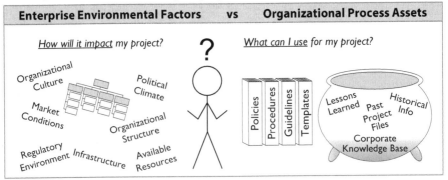

Enterprise Environmental Factors **vs** Organizational Process Assets

Common Tools & Techniques

Expert Judgment – Expertise provided by a group or individual with specialized knowledge or training.

Meetings – Interactive communication tool for the exchange of project information.

Common Outputs

Project Documents Updates – Updated project documentation.

Project Management Plan Updates – Updated project management plan and/or components, modified through change control.

Change Requests – Includes scope changes, corrective actions, preventive actions, and/or defect repairs.

Organizational Process Assets Updates – Updated procedures, guidelines, templates, lessons learned, etc.

Work Performance Information – Project progress data that has been analyzed through the monitoring and controlling processes (see page 11).

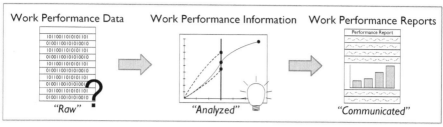

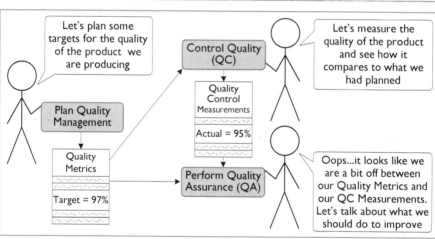

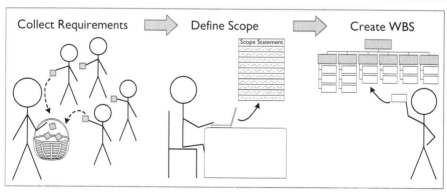

11

Integration

Project Charter

- Developed based on information contained within the project statement of work (SOW), a business case (financial justification), and agreement (contract with an external customer)
- Output of the **Develop Project Charter** process
- Formally authorizes the project
- Signed by the sponsor
- Considered mandatory

Project Management Plan

- Output of the **Develop Project Management Plan** process
- Ultimate "how-to" guide for the project
- Includes all the subsidiary plans
- Includes the scope, schedule, and cost baselines
- Considered mandatory

Change Control

- Change requests are reviewed through the change control board (CCB).
- Change requests include scope change, corrective actions, preventive actions, and defect repairs.
- Scope changes are requests for different functionality or other changes to the project scope.
- Corrective actions are reactive requests to attempt to bring the project back into alignment with the schedule or budget.
- Preventive actions are proactive requests to attempt to reverse a negative trend associated with the schedule or budget.
- Defect repairs are requests to correct an error in the quality of a deliverable.

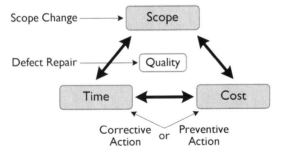

Deliverables

- Output of the **Direct and Manage Project Work** process (see page 11)
- Any unique verifiable product or output from the project activities
- Verified deliverables are an output of the **Control Quality** process (see page 11)
- Accepted deliverables are an output of the **Validate Scope** process (see page 11)

Work Performance Data (see page 11)

- Output of the **Direct and Manage Project Work** process (see page 11)
- Raw data generated by the project
- Becomes a common input to the **Monitor and Control** processes
- Once it is analyzed, it becomes work performance information, a common output

Project Management Information System (PMIS)

- Any tools and systems used to manage project data
- Can include databases, web-based tools, and other software
- Considered an enterprise environmental factor (EEF)
- May also be referred to as the information management system

Close Project or Phase

- Activities concerned with finalizing all requirements for both the product and the project
- PM is responsible for evaluating the scope statement to ensure all work is complete
- Administrative closure includes: transferring the product to the next phase or production, collecting project or phase records, auditing project results, and publishing lessons learned

Group Creativity Techniques

Brainstorming – Used to generate and collect multiple ideas.

Nominal Group Technique – Enhances brainstorming with a voting process to rank the ideas.

Delphi Technique – Anonymous feedback gathered from experts, consolidated and redistributed for discussion, agreement, and/or consensus.

Idea/Mind Mapping – Ideas consolidated into a map to reflect commonalities and differences.

Affinity Diagram – Sorts a large number of ideas into groups for further analysis.

Multicriteria Decision Analysis – Decision matrix that allows consideration of criteria to rank ideas.

Group Decision-Making Techniques

Unanimity – All members agree on a course of action.

Majority – More than half the members agree.

Plurality – The largest subset of the group agrees, even if majority is not achieved.

Dictatorship – One individual decides the course of action.

Facilitated Workshops

- Attended by key cross-functional stakeholders
- Primary technique for defining cross-functional requirements
- Fosters relationships, builds trust, and improves communication
- Examples: joint application development or design (JAD) or quality function deployment (QFD) sessions

Decomposition

- Technique for creating the work breakdown structure (WBS)
- Subdivides the project deliverables into smaller, more manageable components
- May be structured by phase, location, or deliverable
- Hierarchical identification numbering is assigned based on the code of accounts / chart of accounts

Requirements Documentation

- Describes how the individual requirements will meet the business need for the project
- Must be measureable, testable, traceable, complete, and consistent
- Includes business, stakeholder, solution, transition, project, and quality requirements
- Traceability matrix links requirements from their origin through to the completion of the deliverables

Scope Statement

- Describes the project deliverables and the work required to create those deliverables
- Provides a common understanding of the project scope among the stakeholders
- Considered mandatory

WBS

- Graphical, hierarchical depiction of all of the project work
- 100% rule: the lower levels roll up to the higher levels, nothing is left out
- Lowest level of a WBS is a work package

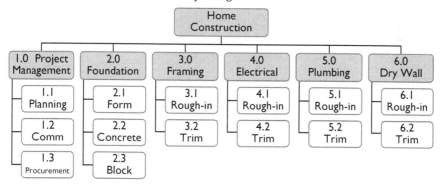

WBS Dictionary

- Companion document to the WBS, providing detailed information on the WBS components

Scope Baseline

- Includes the scope statement, the WBS, and the WBS dictionary
- Component of the project management plan

Precedence Diagramming Method (PDM)

A method of constructing a project schedule network diagram where the nodes or boxes represent activities and the arrows depict the dependencies.

Also called an activity-on-node (AON) diagram.

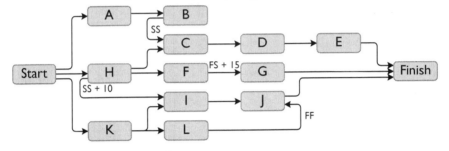

Precedence Relationships

Finish-to-Start (FS)

Predecessor must finish before successor can start.

Example: The books must be printed before they can be shipped.

Start-to-Start (SS)

Predecessor must start before successor can start.

Example: The cabinets must be built prior to being installed. Once the cabinet building starts, installation can begin.

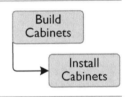

Finish-to-Finish (FF)

Predecessor must finish before successor can finish.

Example: The final construction walk-through must finish before the project supervision can finish.

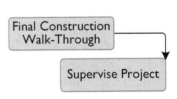

Start-to-Finish (SF)

Predecessor must start before successor can finish.

Example: The new nurses shift must start at the hospital before the previous nurses shift can finish.

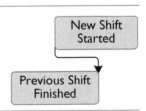

Dependency Determination

Mandatory Dependency – Inherent to the work being done; involves physical limitations, referred to as hard logic.
Example: The books must be printed before they can be shipped.

Discretionary Dependency – Usually established based on the discretion of the project team, based on best practices or experience, may come from outside sources or industry experts, referred to as preferred logic, preferential logic or soft logic.
Example: The screen shots of the new system are to be approved prior to beginning development of the user guides.

External Dependency – Involves a relationship between project activities and non–project activities, usually outside of the project team's control.
Example: The city must issue the permits before construction can begin.

Internal Dependency – Involves a relationship between project activities that are within the project team's control.
Example: The team cannot test a software program until it is designed and built.

Lead and Lag

Lead – Acceleration of a successor activity, only used in a finish-to-start (FS) discretionary relationship. Indicated as a negative number on a network diagram, representing time that is saved.
Example: The photo shoot will take 4 days. The photo editing will take 6 days. Instead of waiting until the end of the 4 day photo shoot to begin editing, we start editing after the first day of shooting. The total duration of the photo shoot and editing is 7 days.

Lag – Delay of a successor activity, has no resources associated with it, may be used in any type of precedence relationship: FS, SS, FF, SF. Indicated as a positive number on a network diagram, representing time that is added.
Example: Completing the application takes 4 days, once submitted the application takes 5 days to be processed, once approved it takes one day to schedule the exam. The total duration from application to scheduled exam is 10 days.

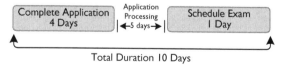

Effort vs. Duration vs. Elapsed Time

Effort – The number of work units required to complete the activity, referred to as staff-hours, days, or weeks, will need to be identified in order to determine the activity duration.

Duration – The total time to complete the activities based on the resources available, does not include holidays or non-working days, referred to as work days or weeks.

Elapsed Time – The calendar time or span required to complete the activities based on the resources available. Includes holidays and non-working days.

Critical Path Method (CPM)

Calculates the early start and early finish dates and the late start and late finish dates for all schedule activities.

Performs a forward pass analysis and a backward pass analysis through the project schedule network paths.

ES + DU - 1 = EF		
ES	DU	EF
Activity Name		
LS	TF	LF
LF - DU + 1 = LS		

Forward Pass
Determines the early start (ES) and early finish (EF) dates.

$$ES + duration (DU) - 1 = EF$$

Backward Pass
Determines the late start (LS) and late finish (LF) dates.

$$LF - duration (DU) + 1 = LS$$

Determines the critical path: the longest path through the schedule with either zero or negative total float (TF).

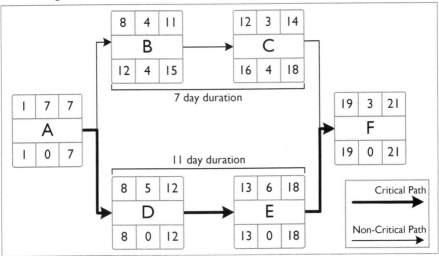

Float

Total Float (TF)

- Measured as the difference between the early and late start dates (LS - ES) or the early and late finish dates (LF - EF)
- Shared between the activities in a sequence (a sequence is defined as the activities between a point of path divergence and path convergence)

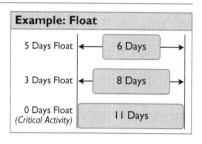

Example: Float

5 Days Float — 6 Days

3 Days Float — 8 Days

0 Days Float (Critical Activity) — 11 Days

- Occurs when there are more than one concurrent activities of different durations
- Represents the amount of time an activity can be delayed without delaying the overall project duration
- Also called float or slack

Free Float (FF)

- Measured by subtracting the EF of the predecessor from the ES of the successor minus 1
- Represents the amount of time that a schedule activity can be delayed without delaying the early start date of any immediate successor activity within the network path
- Only calculated on the last activity in an activity sequence

Schedule Compression Techniques

Fast Tracking

- A technique in which phases or activities that would normally be done sequentially are performed in parallel
- Does not result in increased cost but it does increase the risk

Crashing

- Used if fast-tracking does not save enough time on the schedule
- A technique in which cost and schedule tradeoffs are analyzed to determine how to obtain the greatest amount of compression for the least incremental cost
- Candidate activities are displayed in a crash graph, representing the time saved and the costs increased

Cost

Estimate Types

Rough Order of Magnitude (ROM) – Made early in the project with minimal detailed information. Accuracy: -25% to +75%

Budgetary Estimate – Used to appropriate funds. Accuracy: -10% to +25%

Definitive Estimate – Based on detailed information for each work package. Accuracy: -5% to +10%

Phased Estimate – Near-term work is estimated in detail while ROM or approximate estimates are used for later work. Also known as rolling wave planning. Accuracy: near-term ±5% to 15%, ±35%

Reserve Analysis

- Evaluates the amount of contingency as compared to the amount of risk remaining on the project
- Budget contingency reserve (contingency), managed by the project manager, is allocated for "known-unknowns" (identified risks)
- Management reserve, controlled by the project sponsor, is for "unknown-unknowns" (unidentified risks)

Cost Baseline

- Time-phased budget used as the basis to measure, monitor and control the cost performance, detailing the periodic and cumulative planned value of the work to be completed
- Component of the project management plan
- Typically displayed in an S-curve graph, with the budget at completion (BAC) as the end point

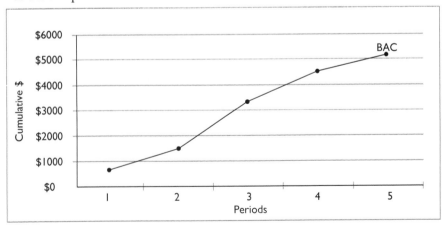

Cost

Planned Value (PV)

- The dollar value of the work planned to be completed to date
- Cumulative from the start date through the status date

Actual Cost (AC)

- The actual money spent on the project to-date
- Cumulative from the start date through the status date

Earned Value (EV)

- Value earned based on the percentage complete of the budgeted work
- **Earned Value (EV)** = budget at completion (BAC) x % complete
- Percentage complete can either be time-based or effort-based

Earned Value Calculations

- **Schedule Variance (SV)** = earned value - planned value
- **Schedule Performance Index (SPI)** = earned value ÷ planned value
- **Cost Variance (CV)** = earned value - actual cost
- **Cost Performance Index (CPI)** = earned value ÷ actual cost

To-Complete Performance Index (TCPI)

- Efficiency ratio comparing work remaining to money remaining
- Work remaining is calculated as the budget at completion (BAC) minus the earned value (EV)
- Money remaining may be calculated using the budget (BAC) or the forecast (EAC) minus the actual costs (AC)
- TCPI = (BAC-EV) ÷ (BAC-AC)   or   TCPI = (BAC-EV) ÷ (EAC-AC)

Forecasting – Estimate to Complete/Estimate at Completion

- **Estimate to Complete (ETC)** is the estimated remaining costs from this point forward, not including actual costs (AC)
- **Estimate at Completion (EAC)** is the estimated overall project costs at the completion of the project including actual costs (AC)
- **Bottom-up EAC** is calculated as the estimate to complete (ETC) + actual costs (AC)
- EAC calculation when there has been an atypical variance is actual costs (AC) + budget at completion (BAC) - earned value (EV)
- EAC calculation when there is a typical (recurring) variance is budget at completion (BAC) ÷ cost performance index (CPI)

Formulas

Term	Formula	Description
Budget at Completion	BAC = total project budget	Assigned project budget
Earned Value	EV = BAC x % complete	Value earned in the work completed
Planned Value	PV = budgeted value of the work to be completed	Assigned value of the work to be completed as of the status date
Schedule Variance	SV = EV - PV	0 = on schedule Negative = behind schedule Positive = ahead of schedule
Schedule Performance Index	SPI = EV ÷ PV	1 = on schedule < 1 = behind schedule > 1 = ahead of schedule
Actual Cost	AC = what has been spent	Actual cost of the work completed as of the status date
Cost Variance	CV = EV - AC	0 = on budget Negative = over budget Positive = under budget
Cost Performance Index	CPI = EV ÷ AC	1 = on budget < 1 = over budget > 1 = under budget
To-Complete Performance Index	TCPI = (BAC-EV) ÷ (BAC-AC) TCPI = (BAC-EV) ÷ (EAC-AC)	Efficiency ratio comparing work remaining (BAC-EV) to money remaining. Money remaining may be based on the budget (BAC) or the forecast (EAC) For TCPI, >1 is bad, reflecting more work than money
Estimate at Completion	EAC = AC + ETC (bottom-up) EAC = AC + BAC - EV (atypical variance) EAC = BAC ÷ CPI (typical variance)	A forecast of the estimated total project spend at completion
Estimate to Complete	ETC = new estimate ETC = EAC - AC	A forecast of the estimated cost remaining to complete the project
Variance at Completion	VAC = BAC - EAC	The difference between the budget and the forecast
Communication Channels	n(n - 1) / 2	The number of communication channels or paths on your project
Three-point Estimate	(O + 4M + P) ÷ 6 (Beta) (O + M + P) ÷ 3 (Triangular)	PERT estimate used for time and/or cost
Lead	Duration A - Lead + Duration B	Acceleration of a successor activity
Lag	Duration A + Lag + Duration B	Delay of a successor activity

Recommended Dump Sheet

As you are preparing for your exam, identify those topics that you may struggle with on the exam. At a minimum, I recommend memorizing the formulas below.

Once seated at your test station write your dump sheet down on the scratch paper provided by the test center. You will receive pencils and a booklet of paper.

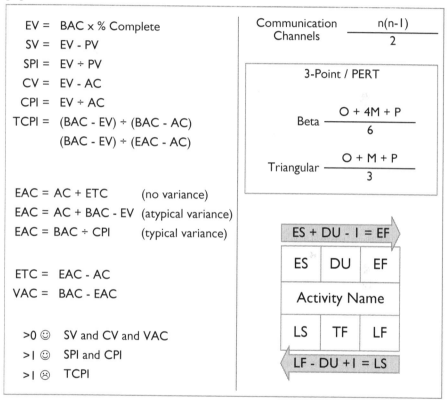

EV = BAC × % Complete

SV = EV - PV

SPI = EV ÷ PV

CV = EV - AC

CPI = EV ÷ AC

TCPI = (BAC - EV) ÷ (BAC - AC)

(BAC - EV) ÷ (EAC - AC)

EAC = AC + ETC   (no variance)

EAC = AC + BAC - EV (atypical variance)

EAC = BAC ÷ CPI   (typical variance)

ETC = EAC - AC

VAC = BAC - EAC

>0 ☺ SV and CV and VAC

>I ☺ SPI and CPI

>I ☹ TCPI

Communication Channels $\dfrac{n(n-1)}{2}$

3-Point / PERT

Beta $\dfrac{O + 4M + P}{6}$

Triangular $\dfrac{O + M + P}{3}$

ES + DU - I = EF

ES	DU	EF
Activity Name		
LS	TF	LF

LF - DU + I = LS

Estimating

Analogous Estimating

- Uses a previous similar project as a basis for the current estimate
- Leverages both historical information and expert judgment
- Used in both duration and cost estimating
- Also known as top-down

Example: Last year's website took three months to develop, I estimate that it will take three months to develop a similar website this year

Parametric Estimating

- Uses a statistical relationship between historical data and other variables to determine a unit cost or productivity rate
- Used in both duration and cost estimating

Example: Last week it took me one hour to mow one acre, I estimate that this week it will take me three hours to mow three acres

Three-Point Estimating

- Uses <u>O</u>ptimistic, <u>P</u>essimistic, and <u>M</u>ost-likely estimates to calculate a weighted average
- There are two variations: beta or triangular (for the exam, assume beta)
- Used in both duration and cost estimating
- You may see different variations of how these formulas are written:

Beta

$$\frac{(O+4M+P)}{6} \qquad t_E = \frac{(t_O + 4t_M + t_P)}{6} \qquad c_E = \frac{(c_O + 4c_M + c_P)}{6}$$

Triangular

$$\frac{(O+M+P)}{3} \qquad t_E = \frac{(t_O + t_M + t_P)}{3} \qquad c_E = \frac{(c_O + c_M + c_P)}{3}$$

t = time   c = cost

Example: With 6 resources it will take 5 days (optimistic), if it is just me it will take 15 days (pessimistic), and if I have 3 resources and it will take 7 days (most likely)

(5 + (4x7) + 15) / 6 = 8 days

Quality

Plan Quality Management

- Determines the quality standards for the project and product
- Creates the quality management plan, process improvement plan, and the quality metrics

Control Quality (QC)

- Evaluates the products or outputs to ensure that they comply with the requirements
- Creates the QC measurements, verified deliverables, and validated changes

Perform Quality Assurance (QA)

- Audits the results from QC (the QC measurements) against the quality metrics to identify areas for improvement
- Considered the umbrella over continuous process improvement

Quality Assurance Tools

Process Decision Program Charts (PDPC) – Links a goal to the steps to achieving that goal, aiding the team in anticipating problems.

Interrelationship Diagraphs – Provides a process for creative problem solving in moderately complex scenarios within logical relationships.

Tree Diagrams – Useful in visualizing parent-child relationships in any decomposition hierarchy.

Activity Network Diagrams – Used with project scheduling methodologies such as critical path method (CPM) and precedence diagramming method (PDM).

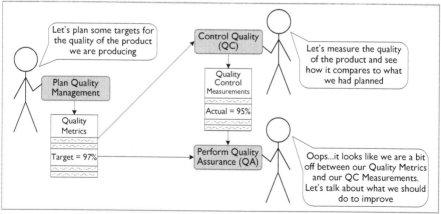

25

Quality

Quality Terms

Quality – The degree to which characteristics fulfill requirements.

Grade – A category assigned to products or services having the same functional use but different technical characteristics.

Precision – The values of repeated measurement are consistent.

Accuracy – The measured value is very close to the target value.

Attribute Sampling – The result conforms or it does not.

Variable Sampling – The result is rated on a scale that measures the degree of conformity.

Special Causes of Variance – Unusual events, difficult to predict.

Common Causes of Variance – Normal process variation, also called random causes.

Tolerances – The result is acceptable if it falls within the range specified by the tolerance.

Control Limits – The process is in control if the result falls within the control limits.

Quality Approaches

Deming – Organizations can increase quality and reduce costs by practicing continuous process improvement and by thinking of manufacturing as a system, not bits and pieces.

Juran – Applied the Pareto principle to quality issues (80% of the problems originate from 20% of the causes) and also developed "Juran's Trilogy": quality planning, quality control, and quality improvement.

Crosby – Created the principle of Doing it Right the First Time (DIRFT).

Shewhart – Developed the Plan-Do-Check-Act (PDCA) Cycle.

Quality Concepts

Customer Satisfaction – Satisfaction is achieved through understanding, evaluating, defining, and managing expectations.

Continuous Improvement – The PDCA cycle is the basis for quality improvement; quality initiatives should improve the quality of the project's management as well as the quality of the project's product.

Management Responsibility – Success requires participation of all team members but it is the responsibility of management to provide the resources needed to succeed.

Prevention Over Inspection – Quality should be built into the products, not inspected in; prevention is proactive versus inspection which is reactive.

Seven Basic Quality Tools

Ishikawa / Fishbone / Cause & Effect

The problem statement at the head of the fishbone is the starting point to trace the source of the problem back to its root cause.

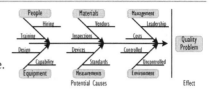

Control Chart

Plots quality results in terms of control limits to determine stability; upper and lower specification limits reflect the maximum and minimum values allowed.

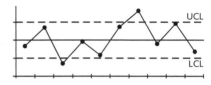

Flowchart

Maps a process, showing activities, decision points, etc, in order to help the team anticipate quality problems and where they may occur.

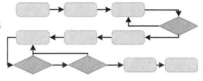

Histogram

Bar chart that shows a distribution of variables, where the height of the bar represents the frequency of occurring.

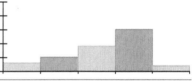

Pareto Diagram

A special type of histogram that ranks causes of poor quality by overall influence in order to prioritize actions.

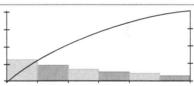

Checksheet / Tally Sheet

Collects and organizes data about a potential quality problem. Data can then be displayed in other charts.

	Criteria 1	Criteria 2	Criteria 3
Attribute 1			
Attribute 2			
Attribute 3			
Attribute 4			
Attribute 5			
Attribute 6			

Scatter Diagram / Correlation Chart

Shows the pattern of relationship between two variables. Uses a regression line to explain or predict how the change in an independent variable will change a dependent variable.

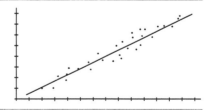

Conflict Management Approaches

Compromising / Reconciling – Implies that one or both parties give up some of their interests in order to come to an agreement -- may be seen as a "lose–lose". *Used when the individuals are not able to reach consensus.*

Collaborating / Problem Solving – Treating conflict as a problem to be solved by examining alternatives; requires a give-and-take attitude and open dialogue; the best way to manage conflict from the *PMBOK® Guide* perspective. *Used when the team is working well together, has a cooperative attitude and open dialogue.*

Forcing / Direct – One person forces a solution on another. *Used when the scenarios involve legal, safety, or ethical concerns.*

Smoothing / Accommodating – A temporary way to solve a problem; focuses on common ground between the individuals and neutralizing the emotion. *Used when the individuals are in a state of heightened emotion that is preventing them from reaching agreement.*

Withdrawing / Avoiding – Removing yourself from the conflict. *Used when the conflict does not impact the project objectives and is not a legal, safety or ethical issue.*

Stages of Team Development – Tuckman's Ladder

Forming – Begins when the team meets and learns about the project, their roles and responsibilities -- at this point, the team members are isolated and not as open with each other.

Storming – The team begins to address the project work, technical decisions, and the project management approach -- the environment can become destructive if the team members are not working collaboratively or are not open to differing ideas and perspectives.

Norming – Team members begin to work together and adjust work habits and behaviors to support the team, increasing their trust.

Performing – For teams that reach the performing stage, they are a well-organized team and are interdependent, working through issues smoothly and effectively.

Adjourning – The team completes the work and moves on to other activities.

Organizational and Motivational Theorists

Maslow's Hierarchy of Needs

Lower level needs must be met before higher level needs are considered. Often depicted as a pyramid with 5 levels: physiological, safety, social, self-esteem, self-actualization.

Herzberg's Two-Factor Theory

Motivators – Give positive satisfaction, arising from intrinsic conditions of the job itself, such as recognition, achievement, or personal growth.

Hygiene factors – Do not give positive satisfaction, although dissatisfaction results from their absence. These are extrinsic to the work itself and include aspects such as company policies, supervisory practices, or salary.

Vroom's Expectancy Theory

Predicts that employees in an organization will be motivated when they believe that putting in more effort will yield rewards. Vroom's theory assumes that behavior results from conscious choices among alternatives whose purpose it is to maximize pleasure and to minimize pain.

McGregor's Theory of X and Y

'X' theory states that people are generally lazy, do not want to work and thus need to be micromanaged.

'Y' theory states that people are self-led and motivated and can accomplish things on their own with little intervention. McGregor believed that people can fall into either category.

Ouchie's Theory Z

Organizations can increase employee loyalty by providing a job for life with a strong focus on the well-being of the employees.

McClelland's Achievement Theory

Need for achievement (N-Ach) is an individual's desire for significant accomplishment.

Those with low N-Ach may choose very easy tasks, in order to minimize risk of failure, or highly difficult tasks, such that a failure would not be embarrassing.

Those with high N-Ach tend to choose moderately difficult tasks, feeling that they are challenging, but within reach.

Communication

Communication Channels

Communications channels formula = n(n - 1) / 2

Where n = the number of stakeholders or team members.

Example: You have identified 20 stakeholders for your project, including yourself as project manager.

To determine the communication channels or paths:

$20 (20-1) \div 2 = 20 \times 19 \div 2 = 380 \div 2 = 190$ *Communication Channels*

Communication Model

The general communication model highlights the key components: encoding and decoding of the message, the message itself, medium, and noise or distractions.

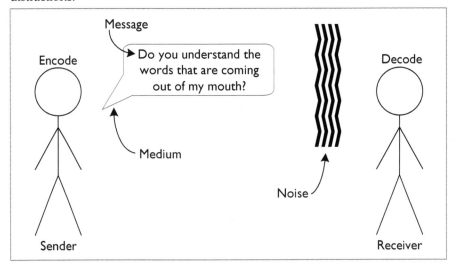

Communication Methods

Interactive Communication – The most efficient method to ensure a common understanding as it is real time, such as meetings or video conferences.

Push Communication – Delivered by the sender to the recipients. While it can be confirmed that it was sent, it does not necessarily mean it was received and understood, such as e-mail or voicemail.

Pull Communication – Provides access to the information however the receiver must proactively retrieve it, such as from a bulletin board or repository.

Risk

Risk Terms

Project Risk – An uncertain event that if it occurs will have an impact on the project.

Opportunity – A positive project risk.

Threat – A negative project risk.

Trigger – Indicates that a risk has occurred or is about to occur.

Contingent Response Strategy – Planned in advance but only used when the risk event or the trigger occurs.

Fallback Plan – Used when the primary response is inadequate.

Residual Risks – Risks that remain after planned responses have been taken.

Secondary Risks – Arise as an outcome of implementing a risk response.

Workaround – A response to a negative risk that is not planned in advance.

Issue – A realized negative risk.

Risk Identification

- Begins very early in the project (presumably before chartering).
- Must involve other people: SMEs, stakeholders, team members, consultants, PMO.
- Is ongoing throughout the project.

Qualitative Risk Analysis

- Prioritizes identified risks for further action by assessing and combining their probability of occurring and the impact on the project objectives if they do occur.
- Often leverages a probability and impact matrix.

Probability and Impact Matrix										
Probability	Threats					Opportunities				
0.80	.80	1.60	2.40	3.20	4.00	4.00	3.20	2.40	1.60	.80
0.60	.60	1.20	1.80	2.40	3.00	3.00	2.40	1.80	1.20	.60
0.40	.40	.80	1.20	1.60	2.00	2.00	1.60	1.20	.80	.40
0.20	.20	.40	.60	.80	1.00	1.00	.80	.60	.40	.20
Impact >	1	2	3	4	5	5	4	3	2	1

Risk

Quantitative Risk Analysis

- Evaluates the aggregate effect of the risks on the project objectives
- Assigns a numerical/quantitative, rating, reflecting impact to the budget and/or schedule

Probability Distributions

- Represent the impact of the uncertainty on the budget and/or schedule
- Continuous distributions represent the data produced by risk modeling and simulation
- Discrete distributions represent uncertain events and may be depicted in either beta or triangular distributions
- Uniform distributions are used when there is no obvious value that is more likely than any other

Sensitivity Analysis

- Determines which risks have the most potential impact on the project
- For example, a tornado diagram, as depicted here, displays cost risk data by range of potential impact

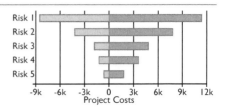

Decision Tree Analysis

- A diagram that depicts a decision under consideration
- Displays the implications of available alternatives

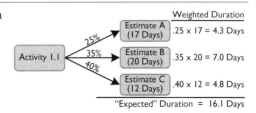

Expected Monetary Value (EMV) Analysis

- Calculates the average outcome when the future includes scenarios that may or may not happen
- Calculated by multiplying the value of each possible outcome by its probability of occurrence, and adding them together for each branch of the tree

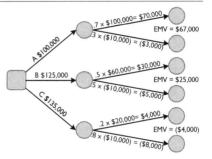

Risk

Risk Response Planning

- Prioritized risks are evaluated for an appropriate response
- Risk owner is assigned to the risk
- Funding, if needed, will be allocated
- Planned risk responses should be appropriate to the level and priority of the risk, while realistic within the context of the project

Strategies for Negative Risks (Threats)

Avoid – Changing the project management plan to eliminate the threat posed by an adverse risk.

Transfer – Shifting the negative impact to a third party.

Mitigate – Reducing the probability and/or impact of an adverse risk event to an acceptable level.

Accept – Acknowledging the risk but not taking a proactive response. Active acceptance establishes a contingent response strategy, passive acceptance takes no action.

Strategies for Positive Risks (Opportunities)

Exploit – Making the opportunity definitely happen through identifying strategies to eliminate the uncertainty.

Share – Allocating ownership to a third party who is best able to capture the opportunity for the benefit of the project.

Enhance – Modifying the size of the opportunity by increasing the probability and/or positive impacts.

Accept – Willing to take advantage of an opportunity if it comes along, but not changing the plan to actively pursue it.

Comparison of Strategies

Threats	Opportunities
Avoid .....is to.....	Exploit
Transfer.....is to.....	Share
Mitigate.....is to.....	Enhance
Accept.....is to.....	Accept

Fixed Price Contracts (risk to seller)

Firm Fixed Price (FFP)
Fixed total price; most common contract type; any cost increase is the responsibility of the seller.

Fixed Price Incentive Fee (FPIF)
Fixed price plus financial incentives tied to achieving agreed-to metrics.

Fixed Price with Economic Price Adjustments (FP–EPA)
Fixed price with a special provision for inflation or cost increases; typically used for longer term contracts.

Cost Reimbursable Contracts (risk to buyer)

Cost Plus Fixed Fee (CPFF)
Seller is reimbursed for allowable costs and also receives a fixed fee calculated as a percentage of the initial estimated project costs.

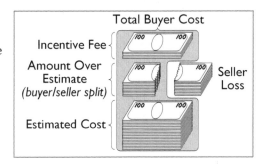

Cost Plus Incentive Fee (CPIF)
Seller is reimbursed for allowable costs and receives an incentive fee for achieving performance objectives; if final costs are less or more than the original estimate, the buyer & seller share the difference based on a pre-negotiated split.

Cost Plus Award Fee (CPAF)
Seller is reimbursed for costs but the majority of the fee is earned based on broad subjective performance criteria.

Time and Material Contracts (T&M) (moderate risk to buyer)

A hybrid type of contractual agreement that has both cost-reimbursable and fixed-price type arrangements. T&M contracts are usually used for staff augmentation, acquisition of experts and any outside support.

T&M contracts can increase in contract value as if they were cost-reimbursable contracts and as such, the organization may add a "not-to-exceed" value to prevent unlimited cost growth.

Stakeholder Analysis

- Identifies all project stakeholders and their roles, departments, interests, knowledge levels, expectations, and level of influence
- Identifies the potential impact or support expected from each stakeholder

Power / Interest Grid

Classifies stakeholders based on their level of authority (power) and their level of concern (how likely they are to show interest).

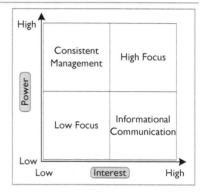

Power / Influence grid

Classifies stakeholders based on their level of authority (power) and their active involvement (influence).

Influence / Impact grid

Classifies stakeholders based on their active involvement (influence) and their ability to effect changes to the project (impact).

Salience Model

Classifies stakeholders based on their power (ability to impose their will), urgency (need for immediate attention), and legitimacy (involvement is appropriate).

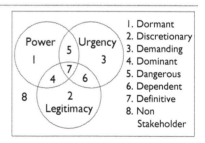

Professional and Social Responsibility

Code of Ethics and Professional Conduct

Applies to:
- All PMI Members
- Non-members who hold a PMI certification
- Non-members who apply to commence a PMI certification process
- Non-members who serve PMI in a volunteer capacity

Aspirational Standards of Conduct – The conduct we strive to uphold as practitioners. Although they may be difficult to measure, these standards are an expectation and are not optional.

Mandatory Standards of Conduct – Establish firm requirements and those who do not conduct themselves in accordance will be subject to disciplinary action before the PMI Ethics Review Committee.

Code Values

Responsibility – Our duty to take ownership for the decisions we make or fail to make, the actions we take or fail to take, and the consequences that result.

Respect – Our duty to show a high regard for ourselves, others, and the resources entrusted to us. Resources entrusted to us may include people, money, reputation, the safety of others, and natural or environmental resources.

Fairness – Our duty to make decisions and act impartially and objectively. Our conduct must be free from competing self interest, prejudice and favoritism.

Honesty – Our duty to understand the truth and act in a truthful manner both in our communications and in our conduct.

Adapted from the PMI Code of Ethics, PMI.org

Professional and Social Responsibility

Code Definitions

Abusive Manner – Conduct that results in physical harm or creates intense feelings of fear, humiliation, manipulation, or exploitation in another person.

Conflict of Interest – A situation that arises when a practitioner of project management is faced with making a decision or doing some act that will benefit the practitioner or another person or organization to which the practitioner owes a duty of loyalty and at the same time will harm another person or organization to which the practitioner owes a similar duty of loyalty.

Duty of Loyalty – A person's responsibility, legal or moral, to promote the best interest of an organization or other person with whom they are affiliated.

Practitioner – A person engaged in an activity that contributes to the management of a project, portfolio, or program, as part of the project management profession.

Other Responsibilities

Maintaining individual integrity – Being truthful, protecting confidential information, reporting violations of ethics and laws, not receiving or giving inappropriate gifts, following copyright laws.

Contributing to the project management knowledge base – Sharing of lessons learned, documenting and writing articles or conducting research on project management practices, mentoring other project professionals, and supporting the ongoing project education of team members and stakeholders.

Enhancing your personal professional competence – Identification of your strengths and weaknesses and planning your professional development activities accordingly.

Promoting interaction and open communication among stakeholders – Balancing stakeholders' interests throughout the life of the project.

Integration Processes

Develop Project Charter (PMBOK pg 66)

Secures authorization for the project to begin, creating the project charter.

Key Output: Project charter

Develop Project Management Plan (PMBOK pg 72)

Documents how the project is going to be executed, monitored and controlled and closed. Incorporates all of the subsidiary plans and the project baselines into the project management plan.

Key Output: Project management plan

Direct and Manage Project Work (PMBOK pg 79)

Performs the work defined in the project management plan to achieve the project's objectives.

Key Outputs: Deliverables | Work performance data

Monitor and Control Project Work (PMBOK pg 86)

Tracks, reviews, and regulates the project to meet the performance objectives defined in the project management plan.

Key Output: Work performance reports

Perform Integrated Change Control (PMBOK pg 94)

Reviews all change requests, approves and manages changes to the deliverables, organizational process assets, project documents, and the project management plan.

Key Outputs: Approved change requests | Change log

Close Project or Phase (PMBOK pg 100)

Finalizes all activities across all of the project management process groups to formally complete the project or phase.

Key Output: Final product, service or result transition

Scope Processes

Plan Scope Management (PMBOK pg 107)

Creates the scope management plan, documenting how the project scope will be defined, validated, and controlled.

Key Outputs: Scope management plan | Requirements management plan

Collect Requirements (PMBOK pg 110)

Documents stakeholder requirements for both the project and the product.

Key Outputs: Requirements documentation | Requirements traceability matrix

Define Scope (PMBOK pg 120)

Develops a detailed written description of the project and product.

Key Output: Project scope statement

Create WBS (PMBOK pg 125)

Subdivides project deliverables and project work into smaller work packages.

Key Outputs: Scope baseline (WBS, WBS dictionary, scope statement)

Validate Scope (PMBOK pg 133)

Obtains final customer or end-user acceptance of the completed project deliverables.

Key Output: Accepted deliverables

Control Scope (PMBOK pg 136)

Identifies any variances between the scope baseline and the work being completed on the project.

Plan Schedule Management (PMBOK pg 145)

Establishes the guidelines for how the project schedule will be planned, developed, managed, executed, and controlled.

Key Output: Schedule management plan

Define Activities (PMBOK pg 149)

Decomposes the work packages from the WBS into schedule activities.

Key Outputs: Activity list | Activity attributes | Milestone list

Sequence Activities (PMBOK pg 153)

Identifies relationships that exist between the activities and documents those relationships in a schedule network diagram.

Key Output: Project schedule network diagram

Estimate Activity Resources (PMBOK pg 160)

Determines the type and quantities of material, people, equipment or supplies required to perform each activity.

Key Outputs: Activity resource requirements | Resource breakdown structure

Estimate Activity Durations (PMBOK pg 165)

Determines the level of effort and the duration for each activity.

Key Output: Activity duration estimates

Develop Schedule (PMBOK pg 172)

Documents all time planning process outputs into the project schedule.

Key Outputs: Project schedule | Schedule baseline | Schedule data | Project calendars

Control Schedule (PMBOK pg 185)

Identifies the variance between the schedule baseline and actual project progress.

Key Output: Schedule forecasts

Cost / Quality Processes

Plan Cost Management (PMBOK pg 195)

Establishes the guidelines for how the project costs will be planned, developed, managed, executed, and controlled.

Key Output: Cost management plan

Estimate Costs (PMBOK pg 200)

Determines cost estimates for the project activities.

Key Outputs: Activity cost estimates I Basis of estimates

Determine Budget (PMBOK pg 208)

Estimates the timing of the project costs across the life of the project in order to develop the cost performance baseline and determine the funding requirements.

Key Outputs: Cost baseline I Project funding requirements

Control Costs (PMBOK pg 215)

Identifies the variance between the baseline and actual costs, determining project forecasts.

Key Output: Cost forecasts

Plan Quality Management (PMBOK pg 231)

Identifies the quality standards for the project and the product, documenting how the project will demonstrate compliance with those quality requirements.

Key Outputs: Quality management plan I Process improvement plan I Quality metrics I Quality checklists

Perform Quality Assurance (PMBOK pg 242)

Audits the quality requirements and the results from quality control to ensure the project is employing the appropriate processes to achieve the project quality objectives.

Control Quality (PMBOK pg 248)

Validates that the project outputs and deliverables are achieving the quality metrics, validates that approved change requests are implemented appropriately.

Key outputs: Quality control measurements I Validated changes I Verified deliverables

HR / Communication Processes

Plan Human Resource Management (PMBOK pg 258)

Develops the human resource plan and documents the project resource roles, responsibilities, and reporting relationships. Also creates the staffing management plan.

Key Output: Human resource management plan

Acquire Project Team (PMBOK pg 267)

Confirms resource availability and obtains the team necessary to complete project assignments.

Key outputs: Project staff assignments | Resource calendars

Develop Project Team (PMBOK pg 273)

Improves the competencies, team interaction, and the overall team environment to enhance project performance.

Key output: Team performance assessments

Manage Project Team (PMBOK pg 279)

Tracks team member performance, provides feedback, resolves issues, and manages changes to optimize project performance.

Plan Communications Management (PMBOK pg 289)

Creates the communication plan, detailing the stakeholders' communication needs and the frequency, format, and content of the project communications.

Key Output: Communication management plan

Manage Communications (PMBOK pg 297)

Manages communication in order to satisfy the needs of, and resolve issues with, project stakeholders.

Key Output: Project communications

Control Communications (PMBOK pg 303)

Provides the current status of the project progress against the baselines to the stakeholders, including variance information and project forecasting.

Plan Risk Management (PMBOK pg 313)

Determines the project approach to risk management.

Key Output: Risk management plan

Identify Risks (PMBOK pg 319)

Identifies the risks (both negative and positive) that affect the project and documents the risk characteristics.

Key Output: Risk register

Perform Qualitative Risk Analysis (PMBOK pg 328)

Prioritizes the risks for further action by determining the probability of risk occurrence and the impact on the project objectives should the risk occur.

Perform Quantitative Risk Analysis (PMBOK pg 333)

Evaluates the project risks using techniques such as simulation and modeling to provide a numerical and probabilistic analysis of the risks and the project.

Plan Risk Responses (PMBOK pg 342)

Determines the appropriate risk responses for the identified risks.

Control Risks (PMBOK pg 349)

Monitors the project risk environment and audits the effectiveness of risk responses.

Procurement / Stakeholder Processes

Plan Procurement Management (PMBOK pg 358)

Documents project purchasing decisions, specifying the approach and identifying potential sellers.

Key Outputs: Procurement management plan | Procurement statements of work | Make-or-buy decisions | Procurement documents | Source selection criteria

Conduct Procurements (PMBOK pg 371)

Obtains seller responses, selects a seller, and awards the contract.

Key Outputs: Selected sellers | Agreements | Resource calendars

Control Procurements (PMBOK pg 379)

Manages the relationship with the vendors, ensuring that the contract terms and conditions are being met.

Close Procurements (PMBOK pg 386)

Satisfies all requirements to complete or terminate project procurements.

Key Output: Closed procurements

Identify Stakeholders (PMBOK pg 393)

Identifies the project stakeholders and prioritizes the project manager's communications and efforts based upon a stakeholder analysis (such as power/interest).

Key Output: Stakeholder register

Plan Stakeholder Management (PMBOK pg 399)

Develops appropriate management strategies to engage stakeholders throughout the project, based on their needs, interests, and potential impact on project success.

Key Output: Stakeholder management plan

Manage Stakeholder Engagement (PMBOK pg 404)

Communicating and working with stakeholders to meet their needs and expectations throughout the project.

Key Output: Issue log

Control Stakeholder Engagement (PMBOK pg 409)

Continual process of controlling stakeholder engagement as defined in the stakeholder management plan.

Qualifications

In order to qualify to complete the Project Management Professional (PMP) exam, professional project managers must meet the following criteria:

Education:

- 35 hours of project management education prior to submitting the application.

Experience:

- With a bachelor's degree or higher, 4500 hours and 36 months of project management experience in a professional capacity within the past eight years.
- Without a bachelor's degree, 7500 hours and 60 months of project management experience in a professional capacity within the past eight years.

Application:

- Approved by Project Management Institute.

Application Timeline

Step	Process	Approximate Time
1	Review the certification requirements, verify your eligibility, and create an account on pmi.org.	1 day
2	Organize and document your project experience. I recommend using Passionate Project Management's *PMP Application Assistant Spreadsheet* (PassionatePM.com/pmp-spreadsheet).	3 days
3	Using PPM's *PMP Application Assistant Spreadsheet* as a reference, complete the on-line PMP application at pmi.org and submit. In five business days you will receive an e-mail with one of three responses: • Your application is approved. Please pay your exam fees. • Your application does not appear to meet the requirements. Please address and re-submit. • Sorry, you have failed to meet the requirements. Your application has been denied.	5 days
4	Log into pmi.org and pay your exam fee. Within minutes you will receive a confirmation e-mail saying one of two things: • Here is your test code and your scheduling instructions. • Your application has been selected for audit.	Immediate
5	If you are audited, complete all audit forms and mail them to PMI. In five days you will receive an e-mail saying one of two things: • Here is your test code and scheduling instructions • You have failed to meet the audit requirements. Please refer to the PMP Handbook for our refund policy procedure.	5-10 days
6	When you have your test code, access prometric.com/pmi to schedule your exam	1-2 weeks

Question-Oriented Tips

- There are certain questions that contain extra information. This information is irrelevant and it does not relate to the correct answer. Beware of such questions and remember it isn't necessary to use all the information provided to answer the question.

- Each question has only one correct answer. You need to select the most appropriate answer. Beware of choices that represent true statements but are not relevant. Be sure to read all the options before you select any one.

- You need to answer the questions from a PMI perspective -- not from your own perspective, which you acquired through experience. Remember that PMI is trying to present an ideal environment for project managers which may be different from your own experience.

- Beware of answer choices that represent generalizations, which may be characterized by words such as always, never, must, or completely; these are often the incorrect choices.

- Look out for choices that represent special cases. These choices tend to be correct and are characterized by words such as often, sometimes, may, generally, and perhaps.

- The correct answer may not be grammatically correct.

PMI Concept-Oriented Tips

- The project manager takes an active approach to the job by not waiting until a risk materializes and becomes a problem. This is an extremely important concept that might affect many questions on an exam. The project manager does not escalate problems to upper management or to the customer before fully analyzing them and identifying options. When answering a question related to what the project manager should do in a specific situation, you should rephrase the question to: What is the first thing the project manager will do given such a situation and given his or her proactive nature?

- Assume that lessons learned and historical databases are available. This might not be true in a real life situation.

- Roles and responsibilities need to be properly defined.

General Tips

- Practice eliminating the completely implausible options first.

- There is no penalty for guessing; thus, do not leave any question blank.

- There will always be those situations where you have no idea what the question is asking. Use educated guessing to select the most appropriate option. Remember, you only have an average of 72 seconds for each question. If you do not know the answer of a question, mark it and move on and revisit it later if you have time.

- Answer the questions based on the *PMBOK® Guide* concepts first, and then consider your experience. If they are in conflict, the *PMBOK® Guide* wins.

Exam Day Experience

- Verify the location of your test center, anticipate driving conditions (such as rush-hour traffic), and plan to arrive at least 30 minutes early. You will need to show ID and your name on your picture ID must match your PMI application.

- All of your belongings, including your cell phone and possibly your watch, will need to be put into a locker. The key to the locker will remain in your possession throughout the exam.

- If you feel you will need a snack or a drink during testing, be sure to leave them on the designated shelf in the testing center lobby. No food, drink, or gum is allowed in the testing room. If you put it in your locker, you will not be able to access it during the test.

- Use the restroom prior to starting your test.

- When you are called to go back to the testing room, you will need to reverse your pockets (if possible), roll up your sleeves, and possibly be wanded. Do not take offense to these actions, as they are meant to protect the credibility of the exam and the testing process.

- For the CAPM exam, you will be provided with two dry-erase sheets and a pen. For the PMP exam, you will be provided with a booklet of paper and multiple pencils. Some test centers will offer you a calculator, others may not. If they do not give you one, ask. They may refuse and have you use the one in the testing mechanism itself.

- The proctor will escort you to your computer. There will be a camera on the room, and possibly one over your computer station. If you are worried about noise/distraction, they have headphones available. Some centers will allow you to bring in headphones, as well.

- When you sit down at your computer, you will first need to acknowledge your name on the screen. You will then have fifteen minutes to complete the tutorial, which should only take you a few minutes. This will give you the time to also write down your memorized "dump sheet".

- Once you begin the test, the question-counter will appear in one corner of the screen and the timer in the other corner.

- If you need to take a break for a drink, snack or to use the restroom, your clock will continue to run on your exam. You will need to sign out of the room and back in to the room. You will not be allowed access to your locker.

- For each question, you have the option to answer the question, answer the question and mark it for review, or simply leave it blank. You can navigate forward and backward through the questions.

- After the last question, you will have a summary screen showing the questions answered and those that are marked or left blank. You will have the option of reviewing all or reviewing just those that are blank and marked.

- Once you have completed the exam, there will be a pop-up confirming you are ready to submit.

- Upon submission, you will first receive a survey and then you will receive the results of your exam on the screen. Acknowledge your results on the screen and then see the proctor for your printed report.

7 Deadly Sins of PMP Prep

In order to pass on your first attempt, be aware of these common mistakes made by people who fail the exam:

1. They **only read the *PMBOK® Guide*** or otherwise fail to properly prepare and understand how all of the concepts work together. The PMP exam is much more than just definitions and processes. It requires a full understanding of how the concepts work together in practice.

2. They assume that **years of project management experience** and/or the **ability to "test well"** will get the job done on the exam. Because the PMP exam tests your ability to apply *PMBOK® Guide* processes to practical situations, many aspirants find that the questions do not necessarily parallel their experience. In addition, the PMP test is not a test you can "logic" your way through, even if you do test well.

3. They struggle with **exam anxiety**. As one of the most common fears, exam anxiety propels the tester into fight-or-flight mode which can significantly impair their ability to understand the questions. Recognizing your anxiety and the signs of escalation and having go-to strategies are highly recommended.

4. They **over-analyze, over-read the questions**, consuming too much time. We are project managers and, as such, we are typically analytical. We tend to add more to a question based on our experience. This can seriously derail progress during the 4-hour exam.

5. They **change their answers** after reviewing the questions. Usually your gut is right. If you have extra time during the exam, do not review all of your questions. I recommend reviewing math questions mainly – it never hurts to run your numbers again. But revisiting all questions, can lead to changing answers. The first answer selected is typically the right answer.

6. They **do not have a memorized "dump sheet"**. Think of your dump sheet as your security blanket. At a minimum it will contain all of your earned value, forecasting, and TCPI formulas. This is not stuff you want to stress about remembering during the exam.

7. They **rush through the exam.** Sometimes it is because people get bored and check-out after a few hours. Sometimes it is because they are stressed about time. Being successful on the exam requires you to balance taking too much time with taking too little time.

Questions or Comments?

I'd love to hear your thoughts, feedback, and/or recommendations on this PMP Pocket Guide. Email me at BelindaFremouw.com/contact

Interested in having me speak at your next event?

I deliver high-impact keynotes and workshops on all aspects of project management: project risk management, practical project management, engaging stakeholders, conflict resolution, and emotional intelligence for project managers. Email me at BelindaFremouw.com/contact

Need additional study resources?

Be sure to check out PassionatePM.com for all of your PMP exam preparation needs.

About the Author

Belinda Fremouw, PMP, CAPM, PgMP, PMI-SP, PMI-RMP, PMI-ACP, is an internationally recognized project management consultant, author, and public speaker. With three decades of project management experience, Belinda has worked across multiple industries, including finance, healthcare, IT, engineering, and government.

She has provided training and consultation to thousands of project managers and organizations globally. The first woman in the world to achieve the original five PMI credentials, she has developed multiple successful project management exam preparation programs, including PMP, CAPM, PMI-ACP, and PMI-RMP boot camps. Her robust exam prep courseware is utilized by hundreds of training companies internationally.

Belinda is the Founder of Passionate Project Management, a learning and development firm located in Phoenix, Arizona.

PassionatePM.com

BelindaFremouw.com

Made in the USA
San Bernardino, CA
06 July 2016